SUMMARY

The Book of Joy Book by

Desmond Tutu & Dalai Lama

The Summary Guy

© Copyright 2017 - Present.
All rights reserved.

This document is geared towards providing reliable information in regards to the topic and issue covered. The publication is sold with the idea that the publisher is not required to render accounting, officially permitted, or otherwise, qualified services. If advice is necessary, legal or professional, a practiced individual in the profession shall be ordered.

- From a Declaration of Principles which was accepted and approved equally by a Committee of the American Bar Association and a Committee of Publishers and Associations.

In no way is it legal to reproduce, duplicate, or transmit any part of this document in either electronic means or in printed format. Recording of this publication is strictly prohibited and any storage of this document is not allowed unless with written permission from the publisher. All rights reserved.

The information provided herein is stated to be truthful and consistent, in that any liability, in terms of inattention or otherwise, by any usage or abuse of any policies, processes, or directions contained within is solely and completely the responsibility of the recipient reader. Under no circumstances will any legal responsibility or blame be held against the publisher for any reparation, damages, or monetary loss due to the information herein, either directly or indirectly.

Respective authors own all copyrights not held by the publisher.

TABLE OF CONTENTS

INTRODUCTION 5

SUMMARY 7

    PART 1: THE TECH WORLD VS. OUR INNER VALUES 7

    PART 2: WE DO NOT HAVE TO DWELL IN SUFFERING FOREVER............9

    PART 3: HAPPINESS IN TWO LEVELS.....11

    PART 4: WHAT MAKES YOU HAPPY?......13

    PART 5: NEGATIVITY SUCKS THE LIFE OUT OF US 15

    PART 6: WHY ARE WE AFRAID?..............17

    PART 7: WHAT ABOUT SADNESS? 19

    PART 8: THERE IS ALSO GOOD IN THE WORLD 21

    PART 9: BEING ENVIOUS LEADS NOWHERE 24

ANALYSIS 26

QUIZ...29

QUIZ ANSWERS 32

CONCLUSION...33

INTRODUCTION

Hello, and welcome to our new summary! In this summary we will talk about *The Book of Joy*. *The Book of Joy* is a book written by Desmond Tutu and Dalai Lama. The two men had difficult lives and decided that it would be best if they could write everything that they know. As we read the book, we can read about many things connect to our lives. We can read about how to achieve happiness, how to deal with things that are in the way of our happiness, why generosity is good, why not being generous is not good, and many other things. All in all, *The Book of Joy* is the perfect story for those searching for a quick way out of whatever they are going through. The knowledge of two men, Tutu and the Dalai Lama, should not be disregarded; the two men certainly gained a lot of knowledge during their lives and have something to say to their readers.

This summary is divided into several sections: the introduction, the summary, the analysis, the quiz (with answers), and the conclusion. The biggest section will be the summary section. In this part we will summarize as much of the book as possible and tell our readers everything that there is to know about the secrets that lie within *The Book of Joy*.

When ready, click on the next page and on the summary!

SUMMARY

PART 1:
THE TECH WORLD VS. OUR INNER VALUES

The first chapter of book opens with a question: even though we are living in the 21st century and technology has advanced to great levels, where is our spirit? Where are our inner values? The author says that since we are so obsessed with our material world, we neglect our spiritual world. We neglect our inner selves. The authors also say that most problems that we face are because of our mistakes and shortcomings. Regardless, we should never stop looking 'inside' people. If we want to live in a happy world, we need to be aware of other people as well and their woes.

A lot of people are in pursuit of happiness. But a lot of people also forget (or fail to realize) that happiness is not something that comes from the outside world. We usually think that whatever happens on the outside will greatly influence our inside. And although that is somewhat true, the real truth is that real happiness comes from the inside outwards. For example, our new iPhone will never make us happy for a long time. It will make us happy for a short period of time and after we 'spend' that happiness, we will again be in pursuit of new happiness. This will only lead us into a never-ending circle of chasing something that we will never catch. That is why material things, regardless of how much money we have, never actually work to bring us happiness.

PART 2:
WE DO NOT HAVE TO DWELL IN SUFFERING FOREVER

The second part of the chapter is about something that some number of people does not want to face: suffering.

Suffering is a part of life. It is something that is inevitable. We need to learn how to deal with it. Other people, especially those very close to us (like our close friends or family members), can be of great help here. With the help of other people, our suffering becomes easier. It is still a burden, but it is easier to carry it if you have someone to help you.

The authors talk about what happens to people if and when they are exposed to a prolonged period of suffering and pain. Suffering and pain suck the life out of us. After a long time stuck in pain and suffering, people tend to become negative and passive. They start to believe that their longer season of suffering is proof that they are just 'meant' to be like that. They live their lives not expecting to move away from the point where they currently are. But this is one of the biggest mistakes that can make. Instead of dwelling in our pain and suffering, we need to believe that our suffering is happening because something good is about to happen in our lives. We usually suffer because we only see what is happening to us, or what has happened to us. We fail to see the 'bigger picture.' There is always a bigger picture, because everything flows, everything grows, and everything has a chance to change.

PART 3:
HAPPINESS IN TWO LEVELS

This part is actually a continuation of the first chapter. The authors say that while some people depend on external stimuli to be able to achieve happiness, others find their happiness at a deeper level. This means that this second group of people looks inside of themselves in order to be happy.

Another thing that is very important for happiness is our mental level. When we live our life only to satisfy our physical needs, our happiness will be short lived. The main reason for this is because our happiness solely depends on materialistic factors.

When people develop a true and genuine sense of affection and empathy toward others, people become truly happy and that happiness lasts for a long time. The main reason and cause of this is because we are created in a way that we should make other people happy. We are not created only for our own happiness, and certainly not for a shallow and temporary materialistic happiness. When we try to analyze our brains, we will come to many interesting conclusions. Some of these conclusions say that our brains are equipped with parts that are dedicated to our well being and generosity. These two parts are also connected. This only strengthens the fact that most of us feel extremely good when we are generous to someone. One of our main purposes is to be generous.

PART 4: WHAT MAKES YOU HAPPY?

In this part of the book, the authors again describe our everyday lives as a race in which we are stuck in a seemingly endless loop of paying bills and taking care of our materialistic pleasures. Because we are in constant pursuit of our materialistic pleasures, we do not have time for compassion or empathy for others. The material world is trying to separate us from one another. Even though we seem to be connected more than ever before, thanks to the Internet and modern technology, the truth is different. Humans are in fact more and more isolated and lonely. This only proves that we cannot live without one another, regardless of how wealthy and smart we become.

There is also scientific proof for this theory. Scientists have discovered that people who are really happy cultivate their happiness with others around them. Happy people want to share their happiness and thus want to socialize. People who suffer from depression tend to be left alone.

But how can we be truly happy?

The authors offer several practical solutions and each of them requires our effort. One solution is helping others around us. When we help others, when we do good, we will feel happy. And if we cannot help others, the best we can do is to try not to harm them.

In the next part of the chapter, the authors talk some more about how to achieve true happiness. They suggest that people should possess happy hearts and happy minds. When people possess happy thoughts, and when people are happy in their hearts, only then will the world be truly happy.

There are many people who are afraid of being genuine. They are afraid of what might happen if they show who they really are. This is a somewhat logical fear because many of us were rejected sometime in our lives, either by our peers or by someone else. But when we are genuine and when we decide to show who we really are, only then we will be able to create trust. We want a friend we can trust. Nobody wants people who are distrustful and fake. The key for a good and long-lasting relationship, regardless of what 'type' of relationship we are talking about, is trust and love.

PART 5: NEGATIVITY SUCKS THE LIFE OUT OF US

The authors say that even though we are in pain, we can still find joy and happiness. The only question is: how exactly do we do that?

The answer is simple: we need to develop strong mental immunity. We need to be mentally immune to suffering. The authors say that much of our suffering and unhappiness comes from the depths of our hearts. Since sometimes we cannot avoid negativity around us (such as when a person very dear to us dies), the best thing that we can do is to choose how we are going to react.

Very closely connected with dark feelings and suffering are destructive emotions. Destructive emotions nurture pain. Negative emotions are a very destructive power. They can drain our precious energy. They can cause mental and even physical pain. Destructive emotions may also be the main reason why some people are sick more often than others. Since negativity and negative emotions can literally destroy us, positive emotions have the totally opposite effect. There is scientific proof that positive emotions and laughing can ease pain. We can see this throughout the world in many hospitals. There are many doctors who realize that 'laughing as medicine' can ease pain and even prolong the life of those who are in the greatest need.

PART 6: WHY ARE WE AFRAID?

Every human being has a fear of something. We fear many things: our bosses, our wives (or husbands), our friends, our foes. Fear is something that is strongly carved into each and every human being. But why is that the case? Why do we experience fear? Not all people have fear of the same thing, that is for sure. But all of us fear something.

Fear is something that follows us from the day we are created. In most cases, fear can actually be very beneficial for our lives. The problem is when our fears become exaggerated, even though the 'danger' that we are facing is actually insignificant.

When we are afraid of something, our fear creates frustration and anger. Anger and fear then fuel two possibilities: we can either 'fight' or 'flee,' depending on the situation. But anger, besides fueling our bodies and minds for imminent fight, also diminishes us from the ability to think rationally. In the end, anger never solves anything. There must be an alternative.

We usually feel anger when we are afraid that we will lose something or that we will lose our control over something. When we feel rejected and frustrated, we become angry. In these situations, it is important to acknowledge our fear. When we are aware what is creating fear within us, we will also know how to react in the proper way. When we react in the proper way, our fear level will not ignite our anger and frustration. There is nothing wrong with being afraid of something and there is also nothing wrong with being angry. But we have a responsibility to the others around us and to ourselves to know how to express our emotions in the right way.

PART 7: WHAT ABOUT SADNESS?

Sadness is a very powerful emotion. We feel sadness for numerous reasons. Sadness can be a good thing; we feel it because we lost something we cared about. We feel sadness when a dear friend of ours suddenly dies. We feel it when someone does something to us that we didn't deserve. We feel it for injustice.

Sadness is a direct 'opponent' of joy. Just like in the movie *Inside Out*, sadness can transform things, making us feel overwhelmed with negative emotions.

The problem is that many people do not really know how to express sadness properly. This can happen for numerous reasons. One of the most evident reasons is that we live in a world where we simply do not 'have the time' to feel sadness or to even try to empathize with others.

But sadness is not necessarily a bad thing. People who occasionally allow themselves to feel sadness are different than others. They tend to be more generous and also have much clearer judgment than those who neglect the need for feeling sad.

People who know how to deal with sadness are also the people who have the most empathy for others. They will know how to recognize it and how to help people around them.

PART 8:
THERE IS ALSO GOOD IN THE WORLD

We all know that the world is filled with many bad things such as wars, famine, sickness, and death. People often think that times are now a lot worse than they were fifty or hundred years ago. They think that past was much better than the present. But the truth is different. The world was always filled with sickness, suffering, wars, and all kinds of horrors. That is just how things are. As long as we live on this planet, things will be like this. But there is also good in the world. And we can see that good all around us. We just need open our eyes.

All of us do many good things every day but since we are used to doing them, we do not perceive them as 'good.' We perceive them as 'normal.' And they are normal, but they are also evidence that there is good in the world. A mother who wakes up every morning before everyone else to prepare her children for school and make coffee or breakfast for her husband is one example. A son who takes care for his old, demented, and sick mother is another. Even though we look at those things as 'little and insignificant,' the fact is that those 'little and insignificant' things often change the world.

Yes, tragedies happen and will continue to happen. But that does not mean that there is not good in the world. And it is absolutely okay if tragedy hits us. This is a clear sign that we are normal human beings. But tragedies can also make us more connected. Tragedies are bad and nobody wants them in their lives but one tragic event can bring many people together, creating a path for deeper relationships.

After this, the authors write about another problem that the humanity faces: loneliness.

Humanity is more and more isolated. We live in a highly connected world, yet we are more isolated and lonely than we were before the "tech boom." We have Facebook, Twitter, and many other applications that we can use to socialize with each other. But among those several hundred (or thousand) Facebook friends, there are very few who are our real friends.

Modern times have brought many good things, but they have also brought many things which are not so good. People are becoming emotionally distant. When something happens to them, they have no one to talk to and no one to ask for help.

They are 'alone.' The main cause of our disconnection from one another is our materialistic nature which suggests that we simply do not have time for other people. We are too busy with things that are 'more important.' Because of this, people suffer from loneliness.

In addition, people often tend to discriminate against others. People create difference based on their race and their beliefs. But the truth is that we are all the same. Regardless of being a Muslim, or a Buddhist, or a Christian, we are all the same. We are humans. And when we become aware of that, we open many doors that were previously closed. We see that there are so many things that actually connect us and do not drive us apart.

PART 9:
BEING ENVIOUS LEADS NOWHERE

In this part of the book, the authors talk about how envy can influence our relationships with others and our own well being.

People envy one another and that is natural. We become envious immediately when we see and 'feel' that others around us have something that 'rightfully' belongs to us. But envy is bad for us in so many ways. Not only does it fill us with resentment and anger toward others, but it also makes us feel guilty. We feel guilty because envy tells us that we could have achieved something that the other person achieved if only we did something differently in our lives. But this is not true. Envy is toxic is because it convinces us to lie. We do not (and cannot) know why someone achieved what they achieved. Maybe they deserved their accomplishment, maybe they did not. Maybe they were more educated and more ambitious. We do not know the real 'reason.'

Envious people are not happy. When we are envious, we are focused on what we do not have, instead of being focused on what we already have.

The best way to combat envy is to practice gratefulness. Being grateful is something that is not natural to us, because we were raised in a way that we only ask for more until we die. That is why gratefulness is something that each of us should practice. We can start small: there is always something to be grateful for. Each and every one of us has something.

ANALYSIS

The Book of Joy, a self-help book based on the teachings of the Dalai Lama and Desmond Tutu, is a book about the many roads that lead to one simple goal: joy.

There are many self-help books in which many authors say that "this is the best method if you want to achieve true happiness." Each of them has a point. Yet how a reader will understand this particular book almost entirely depends on the reader's perception of the world. Since we live in turbulent times, times when people are constantly afraid of everything (even themselves), books like these are more than welcome. People need a "quick exit" and a quick solution for their pain, misery, and suffering.

Desmond Tutu and Dalai Lama did not have easy or simple lives. They suffered. When a person suffers and survives, they will always have something to say about their experiences. If that person came out of their experience as a better person, wiser and changed in any way, the better. These two gentlemen have had many experiences from their lives and they decided to show what they have learned. Some readers may be disappointed when they see that the most important aspect this book is joy, but eventually people will understand that joy is actually what we all are searching for.

How can we live a joyful life? What can we do in order to 'achieve' this? These are questions that each person should answer for himself or herself. This book holds some valuable guidelines that can help us discover what it is that will make us truly happy.

We live in a materialistic world, a world that prevents us from being truly happy. There are million reasons for this and the most obvious one is that the material world forces us to get more and more material things for ourselves. Sorrow, suffering, depression, isolation, loneliness, war, fear of terrorist attacks, and fear of who we might be all prevent us from reaching true happiness. The authors offer some really interesting 'solutions' which we can use and then implement into our lives.

The book is written in a simple, reader-friendly manner, which means this book is for everyone. Knowledge can liberate our minds and show us who we really are, and this book holds some very important guidelines toward that liberation.

Therefore, *The Book of Joy* is a pleasant read for everyone who wants to know if there a way to reach true joy and how to do it.

QUIZ

Welcome to our short quiz! In this short quiz our readers will have the chance to test everything they read about the book in the summary above. Questions are easy, answers are even easier to find, and if you cannot find them in the summary, you can always find them in "quiz answers" section below.

Are you ready to try?

QUESTION 1

Why is important to have friends?

  a) We have someone to drink a bear with.

  b) We have a person with whom we can hang out with.

  c) Friends are an important source of advice and knowledge.

  d) Everything above!

QUESTION 2

Is fear good or bad?

a) Fear is never a good thing. Only cowards are afraid.

b) Fear is definitely a positive thing, because it warns us of impeding danger. But fear is not good if it is exaggerated.

c) If you are a child, then it is okay to be afraid. Grown people are not afraid.

d) It depends on how a person perceives fear. Sometimes fear can be a good thing and sometimes it cannot. It really depends on the situation.

QUESTION 3

"A lot of people are in pursuit of happiness. But a lot of people also forget (or fail to realize) that happiness is not something that comes from outside."

      TRUE   FALSE

QUESTION 4

Being envious of one another is a positive thing because it can fuel our ambition and our willingness to become better and stronger than that person.

    DEFINITELY TRUE!   NOT A CHANCE!

QUESTION 5

"The main cause of our _____ from one another is our _____ nature, which suggests us that we simply do not have time for other people. We are _____ with so many things that are 'more important.'"

QUIZ ANSWERS

QUESTION 1 – d

QUESTION 2 – b

QUESTION 3 – FALSE

QUESTION 4 – NOT A CHANCE!

QUESTION 5 – disconnection, materialistic, too busy

CONCLUSION

The Book of Joy, a book based on the teachings of two modern philosophers and teachers, the Dalai Lama and Desmond Tutu, holds useful advice for our lives. Sometimes our lives are a mess. We live in a world in which we are constantly bombarded with negativity and bad news. Is there a light? Is there a way out? The truth is that things are not always as they seem. Even though we are in the endless pursuit of happiness, we rarely achieve it. The materialistic world impedes our happiness. The only answer to finding true happiness is to look in our hearts and the hearts of others.

The Book of Joy is definitely a book that will intrigue those who wants a quick answer to what is and what is not important in our lives. Deep and thoughtful, this book will keep you glued to its pages until you finish reading it.

Buy *The Book of Joy* today and discover the secret to true happiness!

Thank You, and more…

Thank you for spending the time to read this book. I hope now you hold a greater knowledge about ***The Book of Joy***

There are many individuals just like you who would like to learn about ***The Book of Joy.*** This information can be useful for them as well so I would highly appreciate it if you post a good review on Amazon Kindle where you purchased this book and share it on social media (Facebook, Instagram, etc.)

Not only does it help me make a living, but it helps others obtain this knowledge as well. I would highly appreciate it!

www.amazon.com

We have other summary books available for you as well.

1- Summary – Wheat Belly by The Summary Guy:

https://www.amazon.com/Summary-William-Detailed-Summary-Weight-ebook/dp/B00RIE1Z5K/ref=sr_1_1?ie=UTF8&qid=1486882657&sr=8-1&keywords=the+summary+guy

2- Summary – How to Stop Worrying & Start Living

https://www.amazon.com/Summary-Worrying-Paperback-Hardcover-Audiobook-ebook/dp/B06VVKCLQ4/ref=sr_1_1?ie=UTF8&qid=1491015523&sr=8-1&keywords=the+summary+guy

3- Summary – The Giver

https://www.amazon.com/Summary-Quartet-Complete-Paperback-Audiobook-ebook/dp/B06XZPPN7V/ref=sr_1_1?ie=UTF8&qid=1491540894&sr=8-1&keywords=the+summary+guy

4- Summary - The Hard Things About Hard Things

https://www.amazon.com/Summary-Horowitz-Building-Paperback-Hardcover-ebook/dp/B06Y2WHLKM/ref=sr_1_2?ie=UTF8&qid=1491540894&sr=8-2&keywords=the+summary+guy

Thank you for taking the time to read this book, please give us a good review on Amazon to support us, so we (my team and I) can make more summaries for you!

https://www.amazon.com/s/ref=nb_sb_noss?url=search-alias=aps&field-keywords=the+summary+guy&rh=i%3Aaps,k%3Athe+summary+guy

---

Want to learn how to think wiser and better?

Tips for building business, productivity, investing, smarter shopping, etc.

Check out our website: www.thinkingwiser.com

Facebook page: Thinking Wiser (Just Click)

Made in the USA
Middletown, DE
14 March 2019